ntrolling

Traffic

Controlling Traffic

Text: Jan Anderson
Edited: Anne McKenna
Designed: Karen Mayo
Illustrations: Xiangyi Mo
Reprint: Siew Han Ong

Acknowledgements
The author and publisher would like to acknowledge permission to reproduce material from the following sources: Australian Picture Library/Corbis/Bettmann, cover, pp. 5, 27 top/ Tria Giovan, p. 20 centre; Imagen/Bill Thomas, back cover, pp. 6, 7, 8, 9 top left, 9 top right, 9 bottom left, 10 right, 11 right, 12 top, 12 bottom, 13 centre, 13 centre right, 14, 15, 16 left, 16 right, 16 bottom, 17, 21, 31 left, 31 right, 31 bottom; Getty Image/Hulton Archive, p. 11 left; Photo Edit/ David Young-Wolff, p. 25; photolibrary.com/ Gonzalo Azumendi, p. 23/ David Messent, p. 21 inset/ Naunimes. A, p. 24/ Werner Otto, p. 4/ Ryoichi Utsumi, p. 20 top/ John W. Warden, p. 19 left; photolibrary.com/Age fotostock, p. 18; photolibrary.com/Index Stock Imagery, pp. 22, 30; photolibrary.com/Science Photo Library/Ed Young, p. 26/ US Air Force, p. 13 top right; Photos.com, pp. 19 right, 25 left; Retrfile.com/Burke/Triolo, p. 27 bottom.

The author is very grateful to the following people who gave their time so generously: Andrew Bibby, Russell Coffey, Rob Herweynen, Patrick ('Paddy') Michaelson, John Vogt and Martin Wright. Responsibility for the text, however, rests with the author.

PM Extras Non-Fiction
Sapphire
Animals on the Move
Rolling Right Along
Mobile Days
A Moving World
Controlling Traffic
Make It Go!

For product information and technology assistance,
in Australia call 1300 790 853;
in New Zealand call 0508 635 766

For permission to use material from this text or product,
please email **aust.permissions@cengage.com**

ISBN 978 0 17 011660 2
ISBN 978 0 17 011655 8 (set)

Cengage Learning Australia
Level 7, 80 Dorcas Street
South Melbourne, Victoria Australia 3205

Cengage Learning New Zealand
Unit 4B Rosedale Office Park
331 Rosedale Road, Albany, North Shore NZ 0632

For learning solutions, visit **cengage.com.au**

Printed in Australia by Ligare Pty Ltd
8 9 10 11 12 25 24 23 22 21

Contents

What is traffic, and why do we need to control it?

Wherever we go today, there is traffic. On the roads, we are surrounded by cars, trucks, buses and bicycles. When we are on board a train, there are other trains ahead of us, or behind. In the air, aircraft share the imaginary highways of the sky, as they fly from one big city to another. At sea, there are always ships **navigating** their way to their destinations.

Traffic has to be controlled so that we arrive safely at our destination. Aircraft using the same track, for example, have to be managed so that they are kept a safe distance apart. Roads need signs that tell motorists not to do a U-turn in an unsafe place.

When we control traffic, we also help to keep the traffic moving along. This means that we get to our destination on time.

These cars are in a **traffic jam**. They not only have to wait, but are also wasting valuable fuel and polluting the air as their engines run on and on.

In the past, there was very little traffic to control. One hundred years ago there were only a few cars on the roads, and powered aircraft had not even been invented.

Because there was so little traffic, it could be controlled in simple ways. Traffic police controlled the movement of cars at intersections. They stood in the centre of the road and used their hands to show motorists when to stop or go. They wore white gloves so that their hand movements were easily seen, and blew a whistle if they needed to get a driver's attention quickly.

This photo was taken when traffic police directed the traffic.

With modern technology, we now have many ways of controlling traffic, whether it is on the land or sea, or in the air. Computers **coordinate traffic lights** in an area, so that traffic flows smoothly in the busy direction during **peak hour**.

There are traffic management centres that are never closed, not even at night. They **monitor** the smooth operation of hundreds of traffic lights. Some of them also keep an eye on freeways, using cameras to see why the traffic has stopped.

Many railways are controlled from centres that use computers to change train **signals**, or lower boom gates so that a train can cross a road.

watching freeway traffic at a traffic management centre

At airports, air traffic controllers use a kind of technology called **radar** to track the movement of aircraft both on the ground and in the air. When they know where the traffic is, the controllers can help land aircraft safely at the airport.

Without traffic control, the world would be a chaotic place to live in, particularly with so many of us wanting to go places every day.

This radar aerial is scanning the skies for aircraft that are near the airport.

Traffic on land

Most of the trips we do each day are by road or by rail. On weekdays, many of us use public transport like buses or trains to get to school or work. At weekends, many families use their cars to go shopping, or to participate in activities such as sports matches and dance classes.

Roads

Without traffic control, our roads would be difficult, and unpleasant, to use. Cars and trucks have to share the roads with buses and bicycles, which also have to arrive at their destinations safely.

There are many ways to control the traffic on our roads, and sometimes we use combinations of them.

'No technology' kinds of traffic control

The oldest ways of controlling road traffic use no technology at all.

One of these ways is to have road rules. Some of the rules are shown on signs, such as 'No U-turns'. This sign forbids motorists to do a U-turn in a dangerous place, like on a busy road.

Signs that show speeds, like '50' for 50 kilometres an hour, control how fast the traffic moves along local streets, and make an area safer for children.

Road markings, like special bike lanes or bus lanes, are painted on many roads. They control traffic by directing it to use different parts of the road. 'Transit lanes' tell motorists that in peak hour, these lanes are kept for cars carrying at least two passengers. These lanes flow more quickly than the rest. In this way, road markings help control traffic.

This road has a special bike lane.

Major roads often have transit lanes.

You can also design a road to control traffic. Having a roundabout is one way of ensuring that cars enter and leave an intersection in an orderly way.

This intersection has a roundabout.

Traffic lights

The first modern traffic signals, or traffic lights, were invented in 1912 in the United States.

an early set of traffic lights

Modern traffic lights may have turning arrows.

Traffic management centres

Today, there are hundreds of traffic lights in cities, and in many places they are controlled by computers. These computers make sure that lights stay green for longest in the busiest direction. Groups of traffic lights are controlled together, to keep the traffic moving well, particularly at peak hour.

Did you know?

The first computer system to link the timing of traffic signals in an area was invented in the early 1960s, in Australia.

How a traffic management centre works

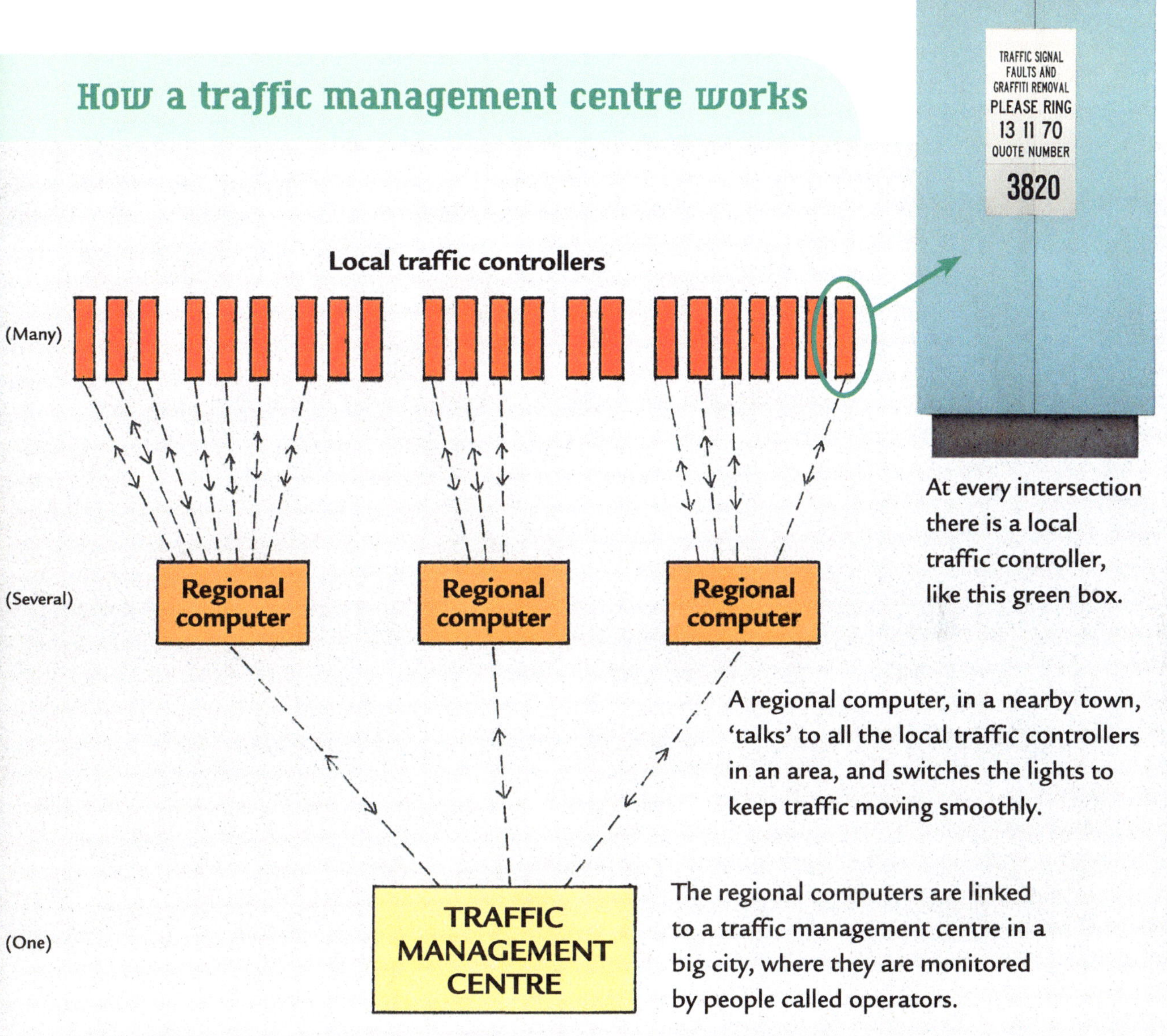

At every intersection there is a local traffic controller, like this green box.

A regional computer, in a nearby town, 'talks' to all the local traffic controllers in an area, and switches the lights to keep traffic moving smoothly.

The regional computers are linked to a traffic management centre in a big city, where they are monitored by people called operators.

For most of the time, the computers control the lights. It's only when something goes wrong, such as a set of lights getting stuck on 'red', that the operators get involved. What do the operators then do?

Every set of lights has a number to identify it. The operator types this number into the traffic management system. They can then change the lights to 'green' and traffic will start to move.

This camera takes moving pictures of a city freeway. The pictures can be viewed by operators in a traffic management centre, to see any traffic problems.

How does the regional computer know which is the busiest direction at the lights?

At every set of traffic lights there are **sensors** in the surface of the road. They are like a loop of wire.

When a car goes over the sensor, a **pulse** flows, and the car is counted. The number of vehicles is sent to the regional computer, which changes the lights so that they are green for longest in the busiest direction.

The sensor loop in this road is placed under the rectangular area.

SmartBuses

Some countries have introduced 'SmartBuses'. These buses have technology on-board to help them navigate. This technology is called a Global Positioning System, or **GPS**.

a satellite

A GPS receives **radio** signals from **satellites** that orbit the Earth, and tells the driver exactly where the bus is.

a SmartBus

Using radio, the driver passes this information onto the bus station. If the bus is running late, the bus station changes the message board at the bus stop to show the correct time the bus will arrive.

a message board at a bus stop

Did you know?

GPS satellites were put into orbit in the mid-1990s by the United States, especially for navigation. GPS systems are used by aircraft, ships, cars, and even bushwalkers – who buy small hand-held GPS systems so they don't get lost!

In some cities, the traffic management centre can help the bus make up time, by changing the traffic lights at the next intersections to 'green'.

Railways

Trains travel along fixed paths – the steel rails that make up the railway network. They have to share busy lines with other trains, so controlling their movements is an important factor in the prevention of accidents. Even when two trains are travelling in the same direction, they must be kept a safe distance apart, otherwise one train could run into the back of another.

It's all about signals and points

Signals and **points** are at the heart of the train system. On the roads, we use traffic lights to say 'stop' or 'go', but **train signals** tell the train driver much more than that. They are like traffic lights and speed signs combined.

Every train signal shows a combination of two different coloured lights, one above the other. Depending on the combination, the train driver is given a different instruction to obey. With three colours of light, and two different groups of them, there are many different messages that can be shown.

A green light over a red one says 'proceed at normal speed' (A), whereas red above green means 'proceed at medium speed' (B). Red over yellow says 'go ahead at medium speed (C), but be ready to slow down in case there's a stop signal (red over red) around a bend ahead'(D).

Points are used to change the direction in which a train travels. They are short lengths of moveable rails that can join different tracks together. The first points were moved with simple levers, but now points are mostly changed by switches, or even computers, that start a motor running to move the points.

The railway points have been moved so that the train goes straight ahead.

The railway points have been moved so that the train goes to the left.

A person called a signaler changes the position of the points. The signal to proceed down a particular track cannot be changed by the signaler until the points are changed for the new direction. This prevents collisions.

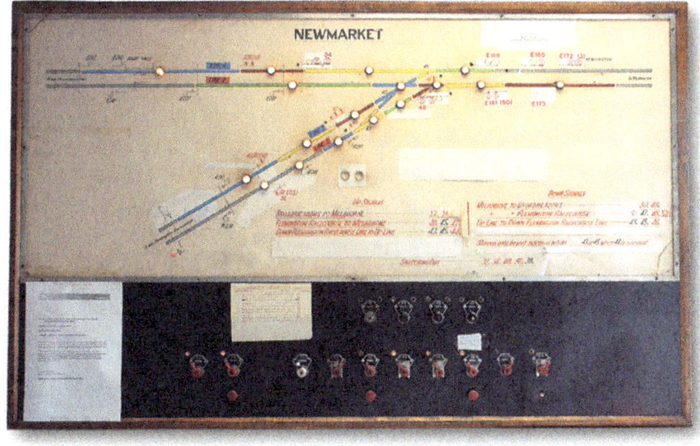

These switches are used to change points.

Did you know?

In Germany alone, there are over 150 000 signals and 87 000 sets of points to control the movement of trains on the main rail network.

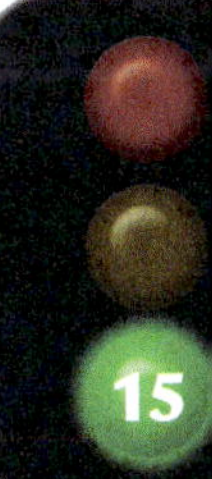

Train control centres

In many cities, computers help to run the rail network.

In some places, a signaler has a single computer to change signals and points. This is done by using a mouse to click the right symbol, such as 'points' or 'signals', on the computer's **display**. The signaler can also lower boom gates by clicking the mouse.

Computers are often used to help control the rail network.

At bigger centres, like the one in the picture below, the system is fully **automated**, and there are many computers.

Every day at a train control centre, a traffic plan is set in the early morning around 3.00 a.m. – before the rail network is busy with peak-hour traffic. The traffic plan is made from the train timetables. The plan is loaded into the computer system. Points and signals are then automatically changed by the computer system.

Every train is given a unique number, or 'ID', for its trip. The traffic plan uses this number to follow the path of the train. The computer displays at the train control centre show all the tracks, and the trains moving along them. The displays also show how the signals and points are set. When a train enters a section of track, the section changes to 'red' on the display, and the train's number is shown next to that section. A 'green' section on the display indicates that the driver has a 'normal' speed signal, and can proceed.

If any change has to be made, for example, if a train is running late, or there's a faulty signal, the signaler operates the control panel manually and fixes the problem, but most of the time the system runs itself.

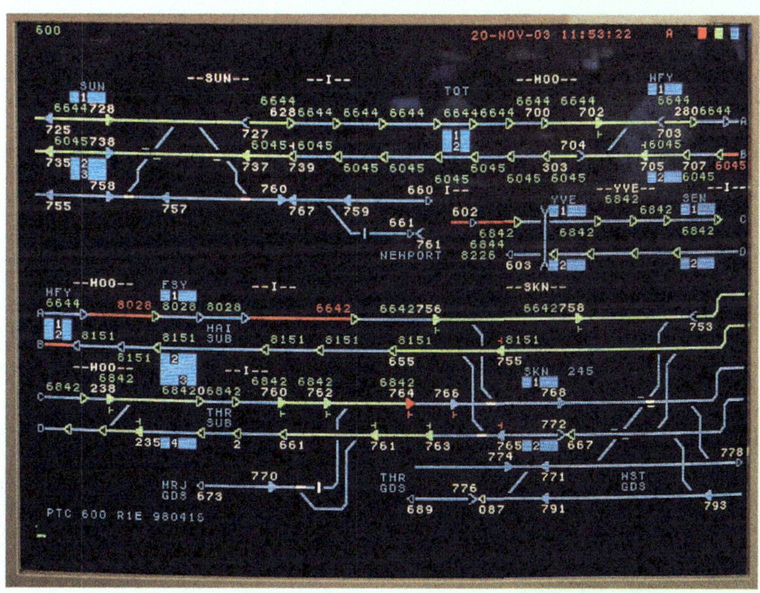

This is a typical computer display in a train control centre.

Did you know?

The train control centre uses radio to tell a train driver when there's a problem, such as a signal stuck on 'red'.

Traffic on water

Ships travel in many different environments, ranging from the open sea to bays, rivers and canals. Even ships that spend most of their time at sea have to come into port sooner or later to unload cargo, or put passengers ashore.

Just like roads or railways, the waterways of the world have to be controlled to prevent collisions, and keep people safe.

The open sea

For centuries, ships only sailed where they could keep within sight of the land, otherwise they became lost. Sailors did not have instruments to find out their position at sea.

Sailing close to land is hazardous, because of shallow water or rocky shores. Many years ago, people built bonfires to warn ships at night about dangerous rocks nearby. Later, lighthouses were built to prevent ships running aground and being wrecked.

Ships at sea have to follow traffic control rules.

Did you know?

'Position' is another way of saying where you are on a map. Sydney, for example, is 33° 53′ S of the equator, and 151° 10′ E of Greenwich.

At first, lighthouses had a simple lamp that was lit at night by the lighthouse-keeper. After a while, lighthouses became reliable **beacons**, with electric lights instead of oil lamps. These electric lights are set to flash on and off at a particular rate, telling a ship its position. To this day, every ship carries a list of lighthouses. Many lighthouses are now automated.

a modern lighthouse

an old lighthouse, with the lighthouse-keeper's cottage beside it

Gradually, instruments were invented to help sailors navigate on the open sea. The early instruments, such as the sextant, could only tell sailors how far north or south they were.

Sailors used to use a sextant (above) and a chronometer (left) to help tell their ship's position.

To measure how far east or west your ship was, you needed not only a sextant, but also a chronometer, which was a super-accurate clock that could withstand the ship's pitching and rolling. With these two instruments, an **almanac** and special tables, a sailor could work out the ship's position.

Today, finding out a ship's position is easy because most ships have a Global Positioning System on-board.

Sailing plan

In some parts of the world, before sailing, a ship's captain prepares and submits a sailing plan to the 'search and rescue' authority. The plan includes the departure time, and expected times to reach particular positions at sea. After the ship sets sail, its position is reported regularly by radio. If no report is received for some time, a nearby ship is radioed to look for the missing ship. By controlling ships in this way, the seas are a safer place for everyone.

Bays, harbours and ports

In shallow bays, **channels** have been made for ships to sail through, so that they are not grounded on sandbanks on their way to the harbour. Ships take their turn to use these channels.

A person called a pilot comes on-board and helps the ship's captain sail up the channel and make their way into the **berth** at the port. The ship is assisted into its berth by a small tugboat that is strong enough to manoeuvre the ship into position.

a tugboat guiding a large ship into its berth

a control tower at a port

At many ports, there is a **control tower** where traffic controllers are based. They control the ships moving in and out of their berths, just like air traffic controllers control the movements of aircraft from a tower at the airport.

Rules at sea

There are international rules for ships at sea. Some of the rules are for overtaking or passing other ships. This is another way that traffic on the sea is controlled.

Rivers and canals

In some parts of the world, barges and ships travel up rivers or canals, carrying many tonnes of cargo.

In Germany, long barges transport coal and other goods along the Rhine.

Rivers were used for centuries to transport goods, before people decided to build canals. Some canals, like the Panama Canal, were built as a short cut for ships. The Panama Canal was opened in 1914. It allows ships to take a 'short cut' from the Pacific Ocean to the Atlantic, instead of going all the way around Cape Horn.

Other canals were built to join rivers, and make a network of waterways.

Because rivers and canals are narrow, traffic using them is often controlled.

In places where a canal goes through hilly country, there are locks. These locks raise or lower ships from one level of the canal to another.

a ship in the Gatun lock on the Panama Canal

How a lock works

The first gate of the lock is opened, to let the ship in, and then the gate is closed. The lock is then filled with water, so that the levels inside and outside the lock are the same. Then the next gate is opened, and the ship sails on through the canal, or into another lock.

Big locks have many traffic controllers to operate them. These workers open and shut the gates and direct ships.

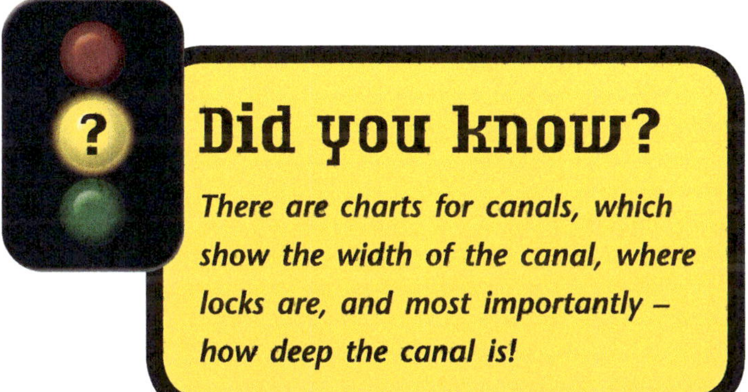

Did you know?

There are charts for canals, which show the width of the canal, where locks are, and most importantly – how deep the canal is!

On the small canals of Britain and France there are locks that you operate yourself. In the past, they would have been opened and shut by a lock-keeper, who lived nearby.

Traffic in the air

Pilots navigate their way on flights like London to New York, with the help of air traffic controllers. They follow instructions given to them by the air traffic controllers.

It would be almost impossible for an individual pilot to communicate with the pilots of all nearby aircraft, because there are so many in the air at any one time. That's why it makes sense to have small groups of air traffic controllers at different places around the world.

Pilots use radio to communicate with air traffic controllers.

Flight plan

Before every flight, a pilot has to prepare a flight plan and submit it to the air traffic controllers. The plan shows the expected departure and arrival times, as well as times to reach particular positions along the way. The flight plan also includes the height at which the pilot would prefer to fly.

Air traffic controllers have a 360-degrees view of the airport, so they can see around them. As well, they have many different kinds of technology to help them in their work.

The job of an air traffic controller is very important because they help keep passengers and crew safe during the flight. Without air traffic controllers, there would be many more accidents.

inside an air traffic control tower

Did you know?

Air traffic controllers are like the traffic police of the air.

This air traffic control tower is where the air traffic controllers are based, and from where they give pilots their instructions.

Where are you, and what are you doing?

Two inventions have greatly improved air traffic control. The first is radar, which is used to track aircraft on a display, and find out where they are.

The second is radio, which enables pilots to talk to air traffic controllers.

Radar

Radar is short for **R**adio **D**etection **A**nd **R**anging. Radar was invented in 1936, to detect aircraft.

How radar works

There are radar stations on the ground. They scan the skies with a special kind of radio signal. When it strikes an aircraft, the signal is reflected back to the radar station. The aircraft is shown on a display that is watched by air traffic controllers. They can see all the aircraft in the region.

a radar display in an air traffic control tower

Radar today

The first radar equipment could only detect an aircraft. Today's radar can find out which aircraft it is, on which flight, and at what height the aircraft is travelling.

Who uses radar?

Pilots do not use radar to see other aircraft around them. Air traffic controllers use radar to see aircraft they are controlling.

Radio

For many years, pilots used Morse Code to communicate with air traffic controllers. They tapped out their message, and sent it by an early form of radio. This was a slow and awkward way of communicating.

an early pilot speaking into a radio

When radio voice communication was invented, it replaced Morse Code, and pilots could talk to controllers on the ground. This was much better, although at times radio reception was very 'crackly'.

Did you know?

Although radio is still used, there is also a system called Datalink, which uses computers to send messages between a pilot and air traffic control. With Datalink, the pilot receives a written message on a computer screen.

a machine used to send Morse Code

A typical flight

Up, up and away!

❶ Air traffic controllers tell the pilot when to commence the flight. After that, the pilot starts the engines, and is given instructions where and when to approach a particular runway.

❷ From the moment the pilot starts the aircraft engines, air traffic controllers follow its path, at first using radar equipment. There is radar equipment at the airport and at radar stations on the ground, for at least the first part of the route.

On route

❸ On some routes, there are radar stations that can track the flight all the way.

The aircraft never goes out of radar coverage. On other routes, there are long stretches without radar stations. The air traffic controllers still have to know where all the aircraft are, to keep giving pilots their instructions. In these regions that are outside radar coverage, it is the pilot's job to find out the position of the aircraft and report it to the air traffic controllers. But how does the pilot do this?

On board the aircraft there are computers that receive radio signals from GPS satellites, and from beacons on the ground. These computers on board the aircraft 'talk' to each other, and together work out the position of the aircraft. They continually update the position.

Because the air traffic controllers are always told the new position, they can keep all the aircraft safely apart. They do this by telling the pilots to use different tracks or heights, or to stay a set time or distance behind each other on the same track.

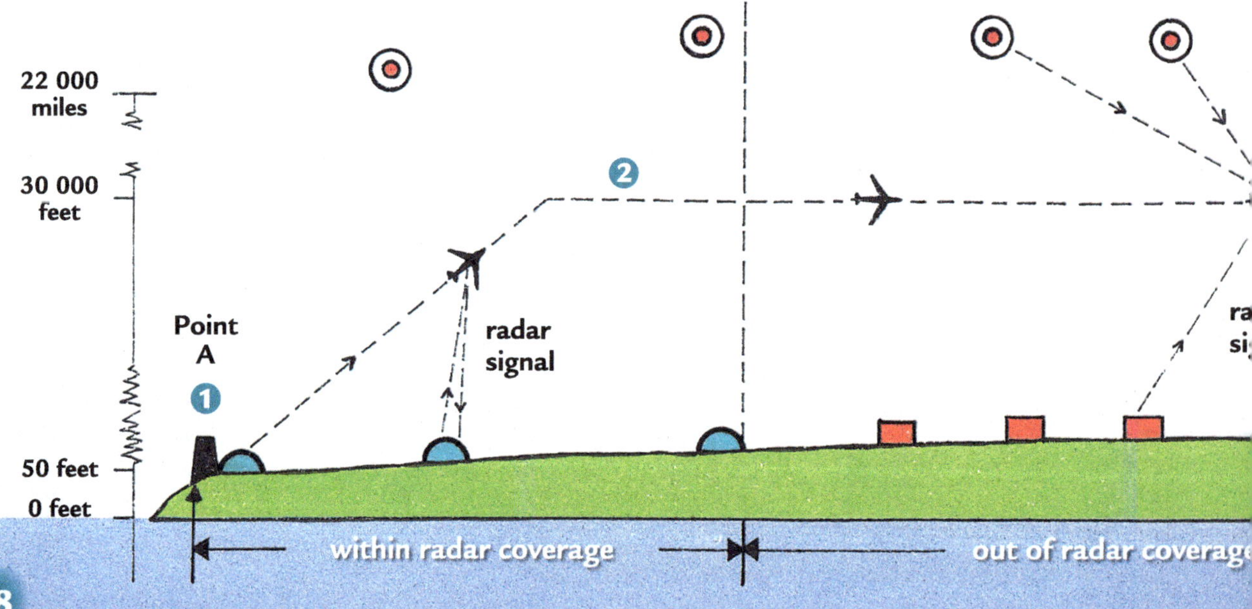

4 As an aircraft gets nearer its destination, it enters airspace that is again covered by radar, and air traffic controllers can see it on their radar display.
The aircraft then starts to descend into the airport.

Landing

5 Landing is easy when the weather is fine, because the pilot can see. In the past, it was impossible to land when visibility was low, or zero.

Now, busy airports in foggy places have landing systems to guide an aircraft on its approach to an airport, and for touchdown. These systems are called Instrument Landing Systems. They enable the pilot to ensure that the aircraft is automatically in a safe position for landing, even when the pilot cannot see the runway clearly. Instruments on the aircraft show the pilot when the plane is not in the ideal position for landing, and the pilot then can adjust the controls to fix this.

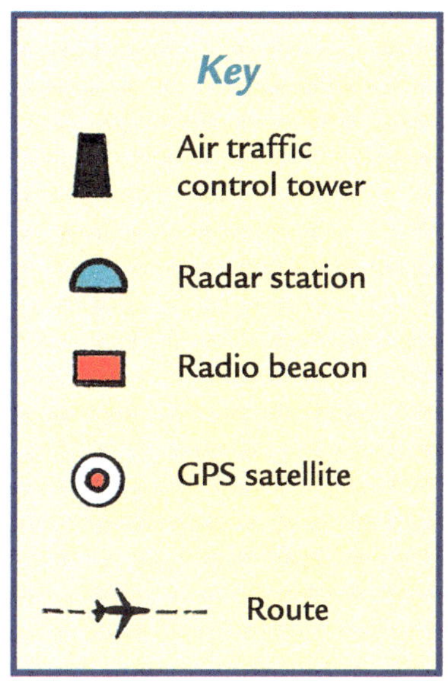

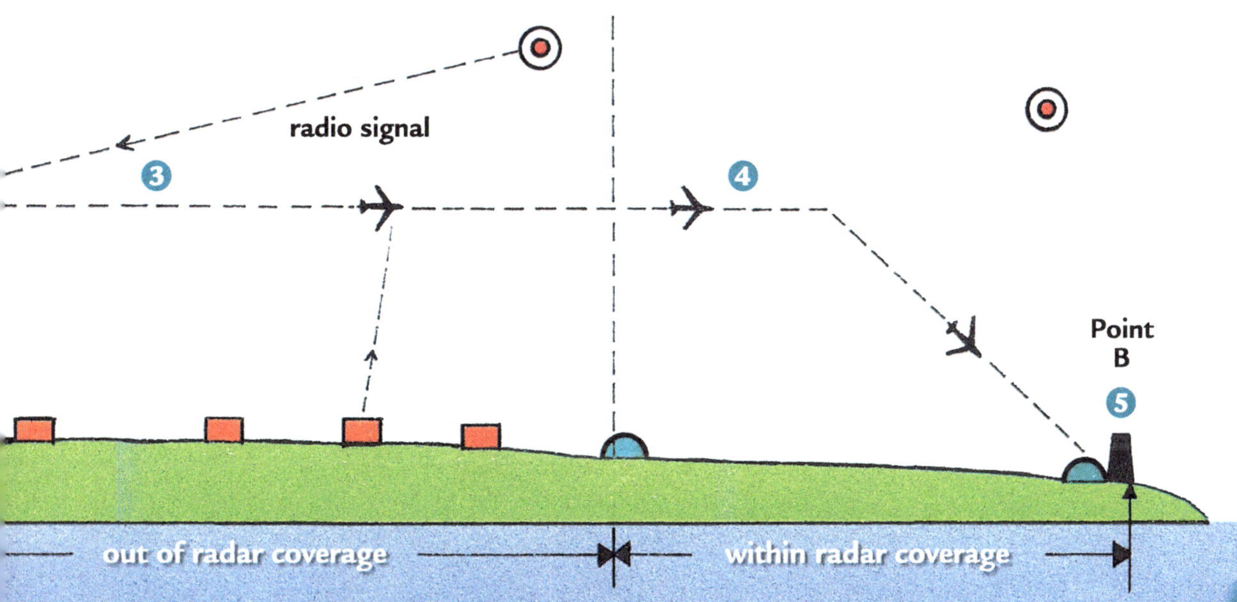

Moving right along!

Next time you sit in a plane or on a train, think about how many traffic controllers and different kinds of technology are at work to make your journey safe, and get you there on time.

Remember that:

- Train trips and flights must be planned.
- Ships' captains and aircraft pilots have to use special charts that show beacons and routes.
- Train drivers and motorists must obey signals.
- There are rules of the road, sea and air.
- The movement of trains along railway tracks, or aircraft along imaginary highways in the sky, must be followed on computer displays.
- Traffic signals have to be set, or changed.

These are just some of the things that are happening behind the scenes when traffic is controlled to flow smoothly and safely!

Glossary

almanac	special calendar for showing the positions of the sun and other stars, the moon and planets, at all times of the year
automated	run by computers
beacon	a fire, or lighthouse, that acts as a signal to warn or guide ships; a radio station whose signal helps ships to discover their position
berth	place where a ship anchors
channels	route through a bay, sea or river that is deep enough for a ship to sail through
control tower	a tall building where people control traffic
coordinate	make two, or more, things work together in an orderly way
display	computer or radar screen
GPS	a device used for navigation
monitor	watch something
navigating	making an aircraft, ship or vehicle go in the right direction
peak hour	time of day when people go to or from work
points	a device for changing a train from one track to another
pulse	short burst of energy, or signal sent
radar	a system that uses a kind of radio signal to find out the position and movement of aircraft, when out of sight
radio	a way of sending or receiving sound through the air
satellite	an object that orbits the Earth
sensor	device for sensing something
signal	an object, or movement, that tells people what to do
traffic jam	when there's so much traffic that it stops
traffic lights	signals for telling cars when to move
train signals	signals for telling trains when to move, and at what speed

Further Reading

Barber, Nicola. *Alpha Books. Transport.* Evans Brothers Limited, London, UK, 1996.

Encyclopaedia Britannica. Fascinating Facts. Transportation. Encyclopaedia Britannica Publications International Ltd, Chicago, IL., USA, 1992.

Harris, M., Harrison, P., Oxlade, C., and Rostron, J. *Illustrated Science Encyclopedia. Transport.* Lorenz Books, an imprint of Anness Publishing Ltd, London, UK, 2003.

Lambert, Mark. *Young Geographer. Transportation.* Thomson Learning, New York, 1993. First published by Wayland (Publishing) Ltd, UK, 1993.

Whitty, Helen. *The Eco Series. Travel and Transport.* Macmillan Education Australia Pty Ltd (in conjunction with the Powerhouse Museum, Sydney), South Yarra, Australia, 2002.